PICTURE WINDOW BOOKS
World Atlases

ATLAS of
Africa

by Karen Foster

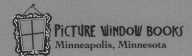

PICTURE WINDOW BOOKS
Minneapolis, Minnesota

First American edition published in 2008 by
Picture Window Books
5115 Excelsior Boulevard
Suite 232
Minneapolis, MN 55416
877-845-8392
www.picturewindowbooks.com

Editor: Jill Kalz
Designer: Hilary Wacholz
Page Production: Melissa Kes
Art Director: Nathan Gassman
Associate Managing Editor: Christianne Jones
Cartographer: XNR Productions, Inc. (13, 15, 17, 19)

Editor and Compiler: Karen Foster
Factual Researcher: Joe Josephs
Designers: Fanny Masters & Maia Terry
Picture Researcher: Diana Morris
Illustrators: Rebecca Elliott and Q2 Media
Maps: Geo-Innovations UK

Printed in the United States of America.

Foster, Karen.
Atlas of Africa / by Karen Foster. – Minneapolis, MN : Picture Window Books, 2008.
32 p. : col. ill., col. maps ; cm. – (Picture Window Books world atlases).
2-4
2-4.
Includes index and glossary.
ISBN 978-1-4048-3880-2
1. Maps–Juvenile literature 2. Africa–Geography–Juvenile literature. 3. Africa–Maps for children.
DT6.7   916 REF
                                                   DLC

Photo Credits:
Paul Almasy/Corbis: 6bl, 27bl; Tiziana & Gianni Baldizzone/Corbis: 12tr; Remi Benali/Corbis: 12bl; Yann Arthus-Bertrand/Corbis:
8tr, 11bl; Richard Bickel/Corbis: 22br; M. Courtney Clarke/Corbis: 21cl; Hervé Collart/Corbis: 19r; Tim Davis/Corbis: 22tl; Nigel J.
Dennis/Gallo Images/Corbis: 23tl; Momatiuk-Eastcott/Corbis: 11t; Randy Faris/Corbis: 24b; Michael Freeman/Corbis: 10bl; Louise
Gubb/Corbis: 10br; Paul Hardy/Corbis: 23br; Roger de la Harpe/Gallo Images/Corbis: 21tl; Martin Harvey/Corbis: 26b; Jon Hicks/
Corbis: 21br, 27br; Rob Howard/Corbis: 9bl, 18tr, 20bl; Kurt/Dreamstime: compass rose on 4, 7, 9, 11, 13, 15, 17, 19, 25, 27; Floris
Leeuwenberg/Corbis: 9br; Charles & Josette Lenars/Corbis: 20br; Gideon Mendel/Corbis: 6tr; Tom Nebbia/Corbis: 18br; Kazuyoshi
Nomachi/Corbis: 8bl, 10c, 12br, 19bl, 26tl; Flavio Pagani/Sygma/Corbis: 23bl; Caroline Penn/Corbis: 21tr; Carl & Ann Purcell/Corbis:
18bl; José Fusta Raga/Corbis: 22tr; Charles O'Rear/Corbis: 20tr; Reuters/Corbis: 18cr; Reza/Webistan/Corbis: 24t; Kim Seidl/
BigStockPhoto: 11b; Paul Souders/Corbis: 25b; Torlief Svensson/Corbis: 28-9; DavidWallPhoto.com/photographersdirect: 26t; Nick
Wheeler/Corbis: 23tr, 27cr; Picture research: info@picture-research.co.uk

Editor's Note: The maps in this book were created with the Miller projection.

Table of Contents

Welcome to Africa

The world is made up of five oceans and seven chunks of land called continents: North America, South America, Antarctica, Europe, Africa, Asia, and Australia. This map shows Africa's position in the world.

Arctic Circle

NORTH AMERICA

Atlantic Ocean

Tropic of Cancer

Pacific Ocean

Equator

SOUTH AMERICA

Tropic of Capricorn

Legend
A legend tells you the title of a map and what the map's symbols mean.

| SOUTH AMERICA | Continent |
| Pacific Ocean | Ocean |

Antarctic Circle

The Antarctic Circle is an imaginary line in the southern part of the world that marks the edge of the Antarctic region.

Compass Rose
A compass rose shows you the four cardinal directions: north (N), south (S), east (E), and west (W).

4

Africa is the world's second-largest continent. It is almost completely surrounded by water. Only a narrow strip of land connects it with Asia. To the west lies the Atlantic Ocean. To the east lies the Indian Ocean.

North Pole

Arctic Ocean

The Arctic Circle is an imaginary line in the northern part of the world that marks the edge of the Arctic region.

Arctic Circle

EUROPE

ASIA

The Tropic of Cancer and the Tropic of Capricorn are imaginary lines north and south of the equator. Places that lie between the two lines are hot and wet.

Tropic of Cancer

Pacific Ocean

AFRICA

Indian Ocean

Equator

The equator is an imaginary line around the middle of the world.

AUSTRALIA

Tropic of Capricorn

Southern Ocean

Antarctic Circle

ANTARCTICA

Scale Bar

A scale bar helps measure distance. It tells you the difference between distances on a map and the actual distances on Earth's surface.

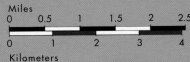

Miles
0   0.5   1   1.5   2   2.5

0   1   2   3   4
Kilometers

South Pole

Countries

Africa is divided into 53 official countries. The largest is Sudan. The smallest country on the continent is The Gambia.

More than 1,000 languages are spoken in Africa. Some languages, such as Swahili, Hausa, and Yoruba, are spoken by millions of people. Others are spoken by only a few hundred.

Africans also use many kinds of sign language. A few languages include clicks and whistles, too.

What's on the menu?

Chad – dried fish gumbo
Egypt – stuffed dates and honey cakes
Ethiopia – cottage cheese and flat bread
Kenya – mashed peas, corn, and potatoes
Madagascar – papaya and mango with vanilla
Morocco – spicy kebabs and couscous
Mozambique – clam and peanut stew
Zambia – fried green banana chips

6

ALGERIA

ANGOLA

BENIN

BOTSWANA

BURKINA FASO

BURUNDI

CAMEROON

CAPE VERDE

CENTRAL AFRICAN REPUBLIC

CHAD

COMOROS

DEMOCRATIC REPUBLIC OF THE CONGO

REPUBLIC OF THE CONGO

CÔTE D'IVOIRE

DJIBOUTI

EGYPT

EQUATORIAL GUINEA

ERITREA

ETHIOPIA

GABON

THE GAMBIA

GHANA

GUINEA

GUINEA-BISSAU

KENYA

LESOTHO

LIBERIA

LIBYA

MADAGASCAR

MALAWI

MALI

MAURITANIA

MAURITIUS

MOROCCO

MOZAMBIQUE

NAMIBIA

NIGER

NIGERIA

RWANDA

SÃO TOMÉ & PRÍNCIPE

SENEGAL

SEYCHELLES

SIERRA LEONE

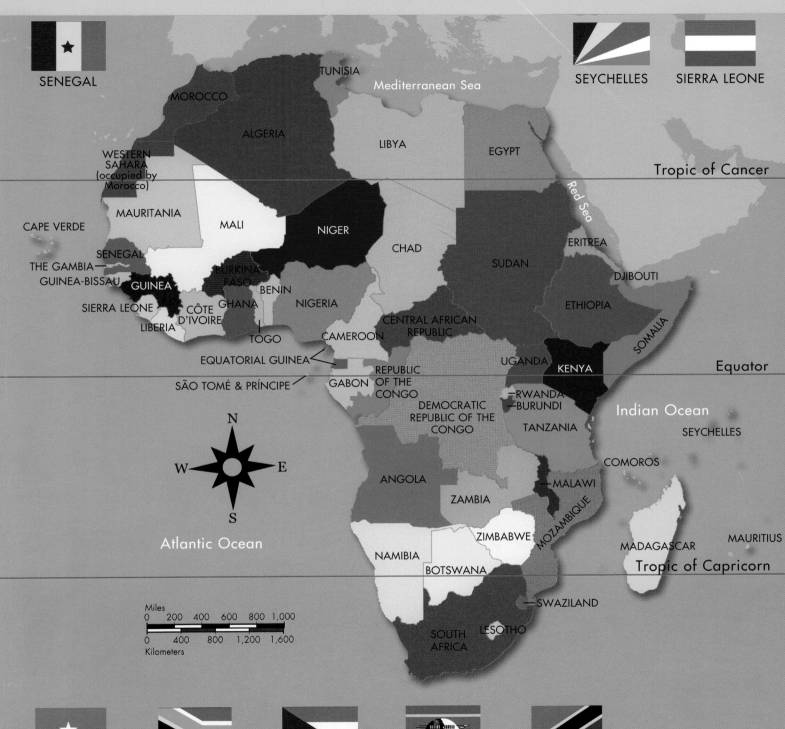

TUNISIA

Mediterranean Sea

MOROCCO

ALGERIA

LIBYA

EGYPT

Tropic of Cancer

WESTERN SAHARA (occupied by Morocco)

MAURITANIA

MALI

NIGER

CHAD

SUDAN

Red Sea

ERITREA

DJIBOUTI

CAPE VERDE

SENEGAL

THE GAMBIA
GUINEA-BISSAU

GUINEA

BURKINA FASO

BENIN

ETHIOPIA

SIERRA LEONE

CÔTE D'IVOIRE

GHANA

NIGERIA

CENTRAL AFRICAN REPUBLIC

SOMALIA

LIBERIA

TOGO

CAMEROON

EQUATORIAL GUINEA

UGANDA

KENYA

Equator

SÃO TOMÉ & PRÍNCIPE

GABON

REPUBLIC OF THE CONGO

RWANDA
BURUNDI

Indian Ocean

SEYCHELLES

N
W E
S

DEMOCRATIC REPUBLIC OF THE CONGO

TANZANIA

COMOROS

ANGOLA

ZAMBIA

MALAWI

Atlantic Ocean

ZIMBABWE

MOZAMBIQUE

MADAGASCAR

MAURITIUS

Tropic of Capricorn

NAMIBIA

BOTSWANA

SWAZILAND

Miles
0 200 400 600 800 1,000
0 400 800 1,200 1,600
Kilometers

LESOTHO

SOUTH AFRICA

SOMALIA

SOUTH AFRICA

SUDAN

SWAZILAND

TANZANIA

TOGO

TUNISIA

UGANDA

ZAMBIA

ZIMBABWE

7

Landforms

Africa has many different types of landforms, including mountains, plateaus, and valleys.

In northern Africa lies the world's largest desert, the Sahara. It is bordered by a band of semi-desert land called the Sahel.

Mount Kilimanjaro, Africa's tallest mountain, rises to the southeast. Most of the rest of the continent is high, flat plateau, broken by smaller mountains and ridges.

Shaping the land

In the Sahara Desert, strong winds and sandstorms form the rocks into interesting shapes.

Rock sculptures in the Sahara

The Great Rift Valley

The Great Rift Valley is a chain of steep-sided valleys in East Africa. It was formed millions of years ago by movements deep within the planet. The valley floor is not flat. It is dotted with hills. These hills are volcanoes. A volcano is a kind of mountain that can spew out lava, ashes, and hot gases from deep inside the earth. About 30 of them are still active.

The Great Rift Valley as seen from the air

The oldest desert

The Namib Desert is the oldest desert in the world. It is also huge. The word *namib* means "endless." The desert is known as a "dune sea." The winds constantly move and change the shape of the desert's large, wave-like dunes.

- The northern slopes of the Atlas Mountains receive a lot of rain and are covered with farmland and forests. The southern slopes are dry and grassy.
- The Horn of Africa is a curved peninsula that sticks out into the Red Sea.
- The Drakensberg Mountains stretch nearly 700 miles (1,120 kilometers) along Africa's southeastern coast.

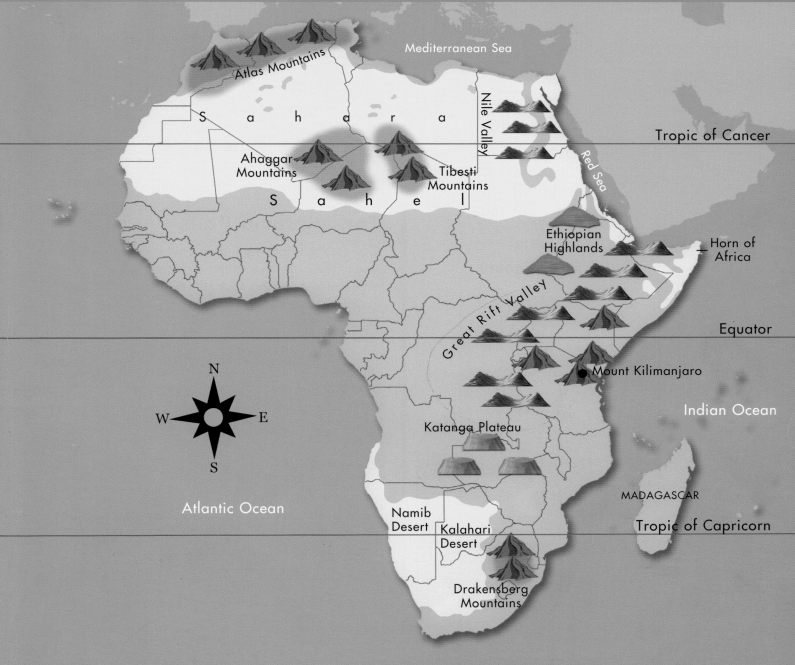

Major Landforms

- ● place of interest
- — country boundary

mountain   plateau   highland   valley

Mediterranean Sea

Atlas Mountains

Nile Valley

S   a   h   a   r   a

Tropic of Cancer

Red Sea

Ahaggar Mountains

S   a   h   e   l

Tibesti Mountains

Ethiopian Highlands

Horn of Africa

Great Rift Valley

Equator

N W E S

● Mount Kilimanjaro

Indian Ocean

Katanga Plateau

MADAGASCAR

Atlantic Ocean

Namib Desert

Kalahari Desert

Tropic of Capricorn

Drakensberg Mountains

The rugged Ethiopian Highlands border the Red Sea coast.

A young goatherder grazes his goats in the Ethiopian Highlands.

Madagascar is the largest island in Africa and the fourth-largest in the world.

The beaches of eastern Madagascar drop sharply into deep water. 9

Bodies of Water

Africa has a lot of water. Four of its greatest rivers are the Nile, the Congo, the Niger, and the Zambezi.

Most of the continent's lakes are on its eastern side. There, chains of long, deep lakes have formed in the bottom of valleys.

The Okavango Delta in southern Africa and the Sudd in eastern Africa are dotted with lagoons.

The Limpopo River

The slow-moving, muddy Limpopo River zigzags through South Africa on its way to the Indian Ocean. The river was made famous in the story "The Elephant's Child" by Rudyard Kipling. Kipling described the river as "the great gray-green, greasy Limpopo River, all set about with fever-trees."

The Victoria Falls

The Victoria Falls lie halfway down the Zambezi River. They are one of the world's largest waterfalls. Water crashes 360 feet (110 meters) over a cliff, causing a sound like thunder. Their African name is *Mosi-oa-Tunya*, meaning "smoke that thunders."

Spray from the crashing water of the Victoria Falls looks like smoke.

Giant sponge

The Sudd is a giant wetland in Sudan. It acts as a sponge that soaks up the flood waters of the Nile River. Because the region is so hot, half of the Sudd's water evaporates (turns from a liquid into a gas) before it can drain away.

One of the Nile's tributaries, the White Nile, runs through the Sudd.

- The Nile is the longest river in the world. It begins in Rwanda and flows north to Egypt, where it drains into the Mediterranean Sea.

- The first non-African person to view Victoria Falls was a Scottish explorer named David Livingstone. He named the falls Victoria, after the then-Queen of England.

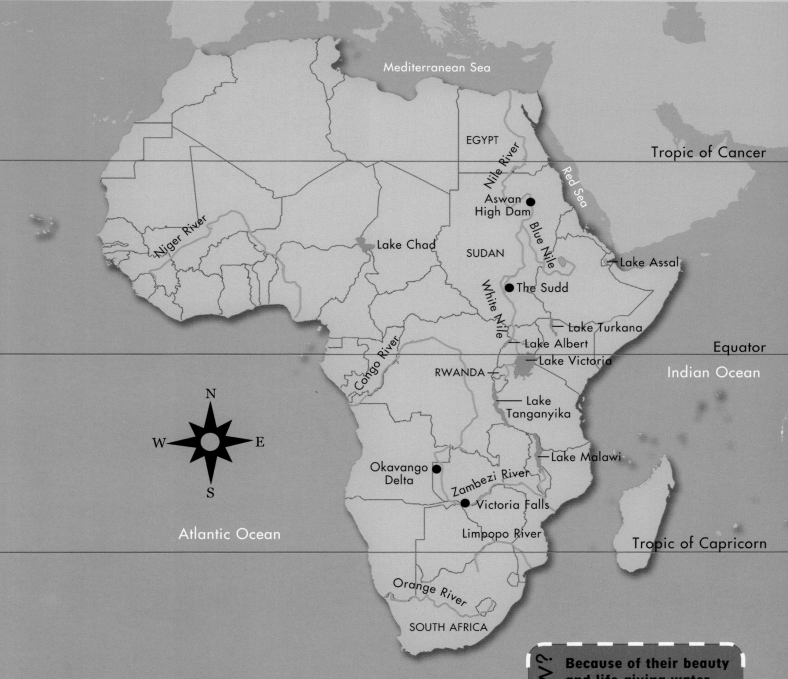

Major Bodies of Water

● place of interest   —— country boundary

 lake   ∿ river

Mediterranean Sea

EGYPT

Tropic of Cancer

Nile River

Aswan
High Dam ●

Red Sea

Niger River

Lake Chad

Blue Nile

SUDAN

Lake Assal

White Nile

● The Sudd

Lake Turkana

Congo River

Lake Albert

Lake Victoria

Equator

RWANDA —

Indian Ocean

— Lake
Tanganyika

N
W ✦ E
S

— Lake Malawi

Okavango
Delta ●

Zambezi River

● Victoria Falls

Atlantic Ocean

Limpopo River

Tropic of Capricorn

Orange River

SOUTH AFRICA

Africa's Lake Victoria is the second-largest
freshwater lake in the world. Lake Superior,
in North America, is the largest.

*Lake Victoria is about 255 miles (408 kilometers)
long and 155 miles (248 km) wide.*

11

Climate

Most of Africa lies between the Tropic of Cancer and the Tropic of Capricorn. Because of this location, much of the continent has a dry or tropical climate.

Climate is the average weather a place has from season to season, year to year. Rainfall and temperature play large parts in a region's climate.

Lightning flashes through the trees during a tropical storm in Africa.

Seasons

In the regions that lie on either side of the equator, the climate is tropical (mountain regions have their own climate). It is always hot there, so instead of hot and cold seasons, the regions have wet and dry seasons. Rain often falls heavily just once or twice during the rainy season, bringing storms and floods.

Hot winds

Strong, hot winds blow across the dry desert regions of northern Africa. Different types of winds have different names, depending upon when and where they blow. Very strong winds can form sandstorms that last for hours or even days.

Sandstorms fill the sky with sand, blocking out the sun.

Climate basics

A region's climate depends upon three major things: how close it is to the ocean, how high up it is, and how close it is to the equator. Areas along the ocean have milder climates than areas farther inland. The higher a region is, and the farther it is from the equator, the colder its temperature.

- The hottest temperature on Earth was recorded in Al Aziziyah, Libya, in September 1922. It was 136 degrees Fahrenheit (58 degrees Celsius).
- Less than 10 inches (25 centimeters) of rain fall each year in Africa's dry climate regions.
- Africa's tallest mountain regions have a cool climate because they are so high above sea level.

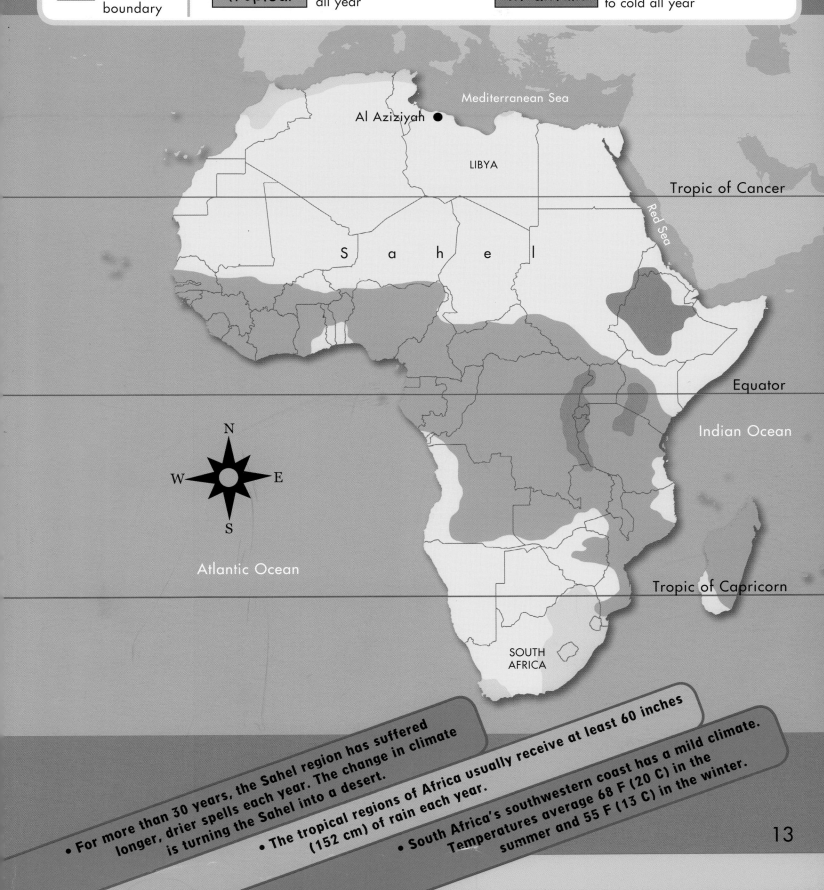

Climate

- ● place of interest
- —— country boundary

dry	dry most or all year with hot summers and warm to cold winters
tropical	wet and dry seasons, hot all year
mild	wet winters or all year with warm to hot summers and cool winters
mountain	wet and dry seasons, cool to cold all year

Mediterranean Sea

Al Aziziyah ●

LIBYA

Tropic of Cancer

Red Sea

S a h e l

Equator

Indian Ocean

N
W   E
S

Atlantic Ocean

Tropic of Capricorn

SOUTH AFRICA

- For more than 30 years, the Sahel region has suffered longer, drier spells each year. The change in climate is turning the Sahel into a desert.
- The tropical regions of Africa usually receive at least 60 inches (152 cm) of rain each year.
- South Africa's southwestern coast has a mild climate. Temperatures average 68 F (20 C) in the summer and 55 F (13 C) in the winter.

13

Plants

Desert and grassland ecosystems cover much of the African continent. An ecosystem is all of the living and nonliving things in a certain area. It includes plants, animals, soil, weather ... everything!

Many African plants have adapted to dry, warm conditions. Trees such as the date palm and the baobab store water in their trunks. Flowers and grasses on the tropical grassland (also called the savanna) have long roots that reach water deep underground.

Some Plants of Africa

desert		date palm	The fruits of the date palm, called dates, grow in large clumps that hang down from the tree.	rain forest	fern	Ferns grow well on the dark, damp floor of the rain forest.
forest		ebony tree	The wood of the ebony tree is black, heavy, and very hard.		liana	The liana is a creeping vine that grows on trees. It climbs to the treetops, where it bursts into flower.
grassland		acacia tree	The flat-topped acacia tree grows on the hot, dry grasslands. Its juicy leaves provide food for many animals, such as giraffes.		orchid	Orchids are the largest family of plants in the world. Their flowers come in many different shapes and colors.
		baobab	Baobabs store water in their huge trunks. The trees' star-shaped flowers smell sweet.	wetlands	mangrove tree	Mangrove trees grow in saltwater swamps along the shoreline and on riverbanks. Their long, twisted roots look like stilts.
		fireball lily	Blood-red fireball lilies produce just one flowerhead each season. The flowerhead may measure up to 10 inches (25 centimeters) across and contain 200 flowers.		papyrus	The papyrus plant, with its tufted heads, grows in the wetlands of northeastern Africa and the Okavango Delta farther south.

Major Ecosystems

country boundary

desert · grassland · rain forest
forest · mountain · wetlands

Mediterranean Sea

Tropic of Cancer

Red Sea

Equator

Indian Ocean

N
W · E
S

Atlantic Ocean

Okavango Delta

Tropic of Capricorn

Animals

Africa is home to a variety of animals. Many are well-adapted to the continent's desert and grassland ecosystems. An ecosystem is all of the living and nonliving things in a certain area.

Herds of zebras and other grazing animals, as well as meat-eating lions and cheetahs, live on the grasslands. Hippos feed on river plants, while monkeys and gorillas eat fruits and leaves in the steamy rain forest.

Some Animals of Africa

desert

	Animal	Description
	camel	The camel stores food in its hump and can survive on small amounts of water.
	scorpion	The scorpion uses the deadly stinger on its tail to paralyze its prey.
	viper	The saw-scaled viper rubs parts of its body together to make a sound that frightens away its enemies.

rain forest

	Animal	Description
	gorilla	Although leaves and fruit make up most of their diet, gorillas also eat insects such as termites and caterpillars.
	ringtailed lemur	The ringtailed lemur lives only on the island of Madagascar.
	mandrill	The mandrill is a large monkey found only in Africa. It has thick blue and purple ridges alongside its bright-red nose.

grassland

	Animal	Description
	cheetah	The cheetah is the fastest land animal. It can catch its prey in less than a minute.
	impala	Impalas are light on their feet. They jump up and race for cover when wild cats come near.
	zebra	Zebras have striped coats that help them stay hidden behind trees and bushes.
	lion	Lions live in groups called prides. Up to 40 lions may live in a pride.
	hippopotamus	The hippopotamus (hippo) is the second-heaviest land mammal (after the elephant).
	wildebeest	Wildebeest travel hundreds of miles each year in search of grass and water.
	giraffe	Found only on the African grasslands, giraffes are the tallest land animals.

16

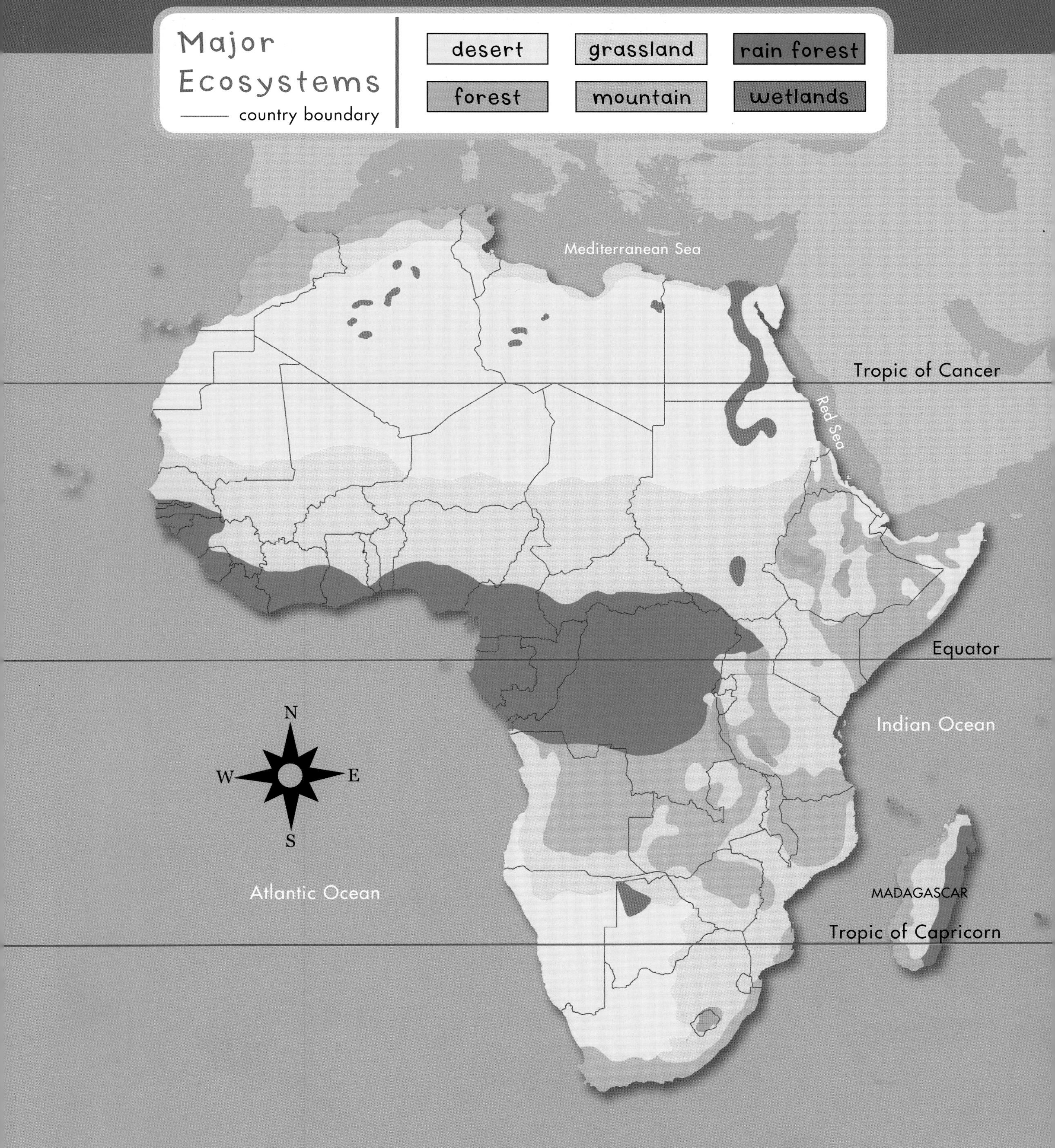

Major Ecosystems
—— country boundary

desert grassland rain forest
forest mountain wetlands

Mediterranean Sea

Tropic of Cancer

Red Sea

N
W   E
S

Equator

Indian Ocean

Atlantic Ocean

MADAGASCAR

Tropic of Capricorn

17

Population

Africa is a continent of young people. Almost half of the population is under 15 years of age. The population in Africa is growing faster than any other continent's population.

Many Africans live in big, bustling cities. Others live in small villages where people must walk for miles to get water.

Health and disease

Food shortages and life-threatening diseases such as cholera, malaria, and HIV/AIDS are common in many parts of Africa. Good health care is not available for all Africans. As a result, people in many African countries cannot expect to live long lives. In Niger, for example, the average life expectancy is 44. In Malawi, it's only 43.

Big cities

There are more than 50 African cities with populations greater than 1 million, including Algiers, Algeria; Casablanca, Morocco; and Cape Town, South Africa.

Nairobi is the capital of Kenya. With more than 2 million people, it's also a large business center. Modern office buildings and hotels are set on wide, tree-lined streets.

Nairobi, Kenya

The Nigerian city of **Lagos** is growing amazingly fast. Now Africa's second-most populated city, Lagos is soon expected to be one of the world's top five biggest cities.

Lagos, Nigeria

Cairo, the capital of Egypt, is the most populated city in Africa. Almost 10 million people live there. Many of them live in crowded, run-down housing.

Cairo, Egypt

- Nigeria has more people than any other country in Africa.
- Namibia averages just five people per square mile.
- Many people live in the Great Lakes region (Burundi, Kenya, Rwanda, Tanzania, and Uganda). It has some of Africa's best farmland, which provides jobs and food.

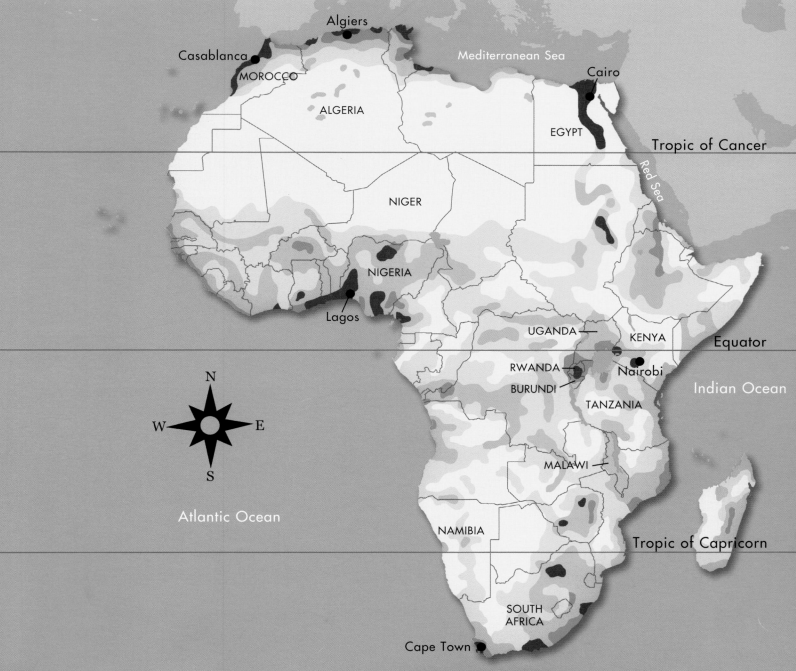

People per Square Mile

less than **5**

5-25

25-125

125-250

more than **250**

● place of interest
—— country boundary

Algiers

Casablanca

MOROCCO

Mediterranean Sea

Cairo

ALGERIA

EGYPT

Tropic of Cancer

Red Sea

NIGER

NIGERIA

Lagos

UGANDA —

KENYA

Equator

RWANDA —

Nairobi

BURUNDI

Indian Ocean

TANZANIA

MALAWI —

N
W E
S

Atlantic Ocean

NAMIBIA

Tropic of Capricorn

SOUTH
AFRICA

Cape Town

People often live
around green oases
on the edges of the
African deserts.

*An oasis in
northwestern Africa*

The Zulu people of Africa
have the largest population of
any African group. In the 19th
century, their kingdom covered
most of South Africa.

Zulu tribespeople

19

People and Customs

Africa is a land of many different cultures and traditions. The very first people on Earth likely came from the African continent.

Much of the continent is made up of several thousand groups of Native Africans. These are people whose ancestors lived only in Africa.

Many people of Arab and European backgrounds also live in Africa, especially in the northern and southern regions. Their mark can be seen in the regions' art, food, religion, buildings, and music.

Home decorating

In southern Africa, the Ndebele people paint their mud houses with bold colors and designs. The pictures are a type of language. They tell visitors about the family's values and how proud the family is to be Ndebele.

A brightly painted Ndebele mud house

The Maasai

The Maasai people of eastern Africa herd cattle, goats, and sheep across the grasslands. They live on the meat, milk, and blood from their cattle. The Maasai are well known for their beautiful beadwork.

Maasai tribesmen wear red to scare off lions, cheetahs, and other wild cats.

Dogon dancers

The Dogon people live on the western edge of the Sahara Desert. They are famous for their stilt dancers, who pretend to be long-legged birds.

Dogon stilt dancers

Celebrations

Village ceremonies are an important part of country life throughout Africa. People celebrate family events as well as the first rains of the growing season, the planting of crops, and harvest time.

Lesson for life

The San (or Bushmen) people of southern Africa must hunt for much of their food. Small boys learn all about hunting from their fathers, uncles, and other adults in the tribe.

San children play a game to learn important hunting skills.

Family living

In Ghana, the Ashanti people build farmhouses in the shape of a big square, with an open yard in the middle. All members of a family live together, including grandparents, uncles, and aunts. In some parts of Africa, the whole village may live like a single family.

Ashanti families live and work together.

School days

In Africa, there aren't enough schools for everyone, especially in poor areas. In the countryside, children must often walk for several hours to reach the nearest school.

Outdoor classrooms are common in many parts of Africa.

South Africa

South Africa is home to a mixture of people from different backgrounds, including British, Dutch, Malaysian, and many Native African tribes. A number of people who live there are of mixed race.

Many people enjoy South Africa's sandy beaches.

Postcard Places

Africa has many areas of great natural beauty. There are also large, modern cities. Old and new ways of life can be found all over the continent. Hundreds of different peoples and their customs make Africa an amazing place.

Luxor

Mount Kilimanjaro, in Tanzania, is a favorite tourist spot. Each year, thousands come to enjoy breathtaking views from the peak, or mountaintop.

Kilimanjaro

Many tourists to Egypt visit the ancient cities on the Nile River. The Egyptian temples of Luxor are thousands of years old.

- Fez
- Marrakech
- Giza
- Luxor
- Mount Kilimanjaro
- Zanzibar
- Kruger National Park

Marrakech

The markets in Marrakech, Morocco, offer every kind of dyed wool and goatskin.

The Kruger National Park in South Africa is a popular tourist attraction.

Come to Zanzibar

Kruger National Park

The island of Zanzibar lies in the Indian Ocean, off the coast of Tanzania. It is famous for its Arabic buildings and its white sand beaches. It also produces large amounts of cloves and other spices.

Carpet market

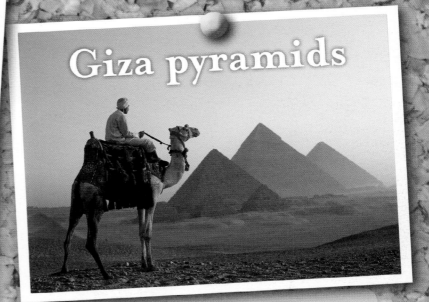
Giza pyramids

In the town of Fez, Morocco, vendors spread out their carpets in the main square for customers to look at.

The pyramids of Giza, in Egypt, were built 4,500 years ago as tombs for Egyptian kings. The largest pyramid is made of about 2 million blocks of stone!

Growing and Making

Africa has a lot of natural resources, including diamonds, gold, and oil. Much of Africa's mining and oil drilling is done in desert and mountain areas.

Africa is still developing its factories and industries so that it can make the most of its natural resources.

Many African farmers have small pieces of land and use simple farm tools. But machines are becoming more and more common. Africa's coffee, cotton, peanuts, and cacao beans are sold all over the world.

In many parts of Egypt, crops are still harvested without the help of machines.

Waters of the Nile River

Life in northeastern Africa would be impossible without the Nile River. It provides water for the farmland along its banks. Crops of wheat, dates, and cotton grow well there.

Diamonds

Diamonds are the hardest gemstones in the world. They are used as cutting tools in industry. They are also shaped and polished to make jewelry. The richest diamond mines in the world are found in the Republic of the Congo, the Democratic Republic of the Congo, Botswana, Namibia, and South Africa.

Diamonds can be cut into different shapes.

- Côte d'Ivoire is among the world's leading producers of cacao beans. Cacao trees are grown on huge farms. The trees' seeds, or beans, are crushed to make cocoa, the main ingredient of chocolate.

- Cotton is grown in many parts of Africa, but the finest cotton is made in Egypt.

- Nigeria is the biggest oil producer in Africa.

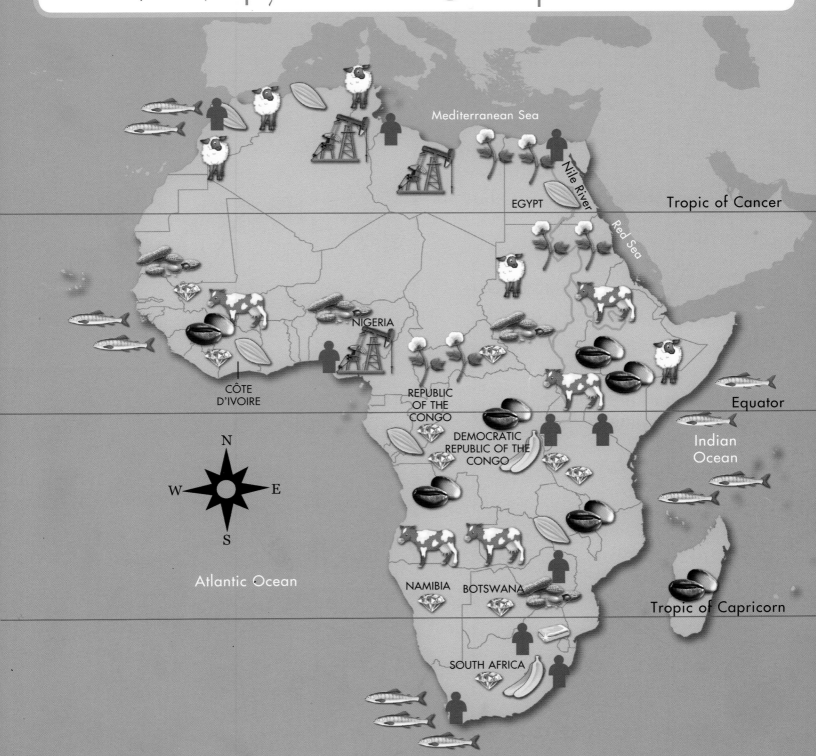

Major Natural Resources, Land Use, and Industry

—— country boundary

Oil Fishing Tourism

Farming cacao peanuts cotton bananas coffee

Mining diamonds gold

Ranching cattle sheep

Mediterranean Sea

Tropic of Cancer

EGYPT

Nile River

Red Sea

NIGERIA

CÔTE D'IVOIRE

REPUBLIC OF THE CONGO

DEMOCRATIC REPUBLIC OF THE CONGO

Equator

Indian Ocean

Atlantic Ocean

NAMIBIA BOTSWANA

Tropic of Capricorn

SOUTH AFRICA

N
W E
S

25

Transportation

Many cities and towns in Africa are great distances apart. Because few people can afford to travel by airplane, many travel by bus or motorcycle. Walking is still the way most Africans get around.

Within major cities, people travel on modern highways. Throughout much of the continent, however, roads are often dirt tracks that flood in the rainy season.

There are busy ports along Africa's coasts. But only a few inland waterways are used for transportation. Thick jungles block many rivers, and some waterways become too shallow in the dry season.

The Suez Canal

The Suez Canal is a man-made waterway in Egypt that connects the Mediterranean Sea and the Red Sea. Opened in 1869, the canal saves ships time and money. Without it, ships would have to sail around the southern tip of Africa to get from one sea to the other.

Camel crossing

Camels have been used for transportation across African deserts for thousands of years. Their wide, flat hooves help them walk on sand without sinking. Camels also store food in their humps and can go for days without water. Today, trucks and small planes are also used to cross the deserts.

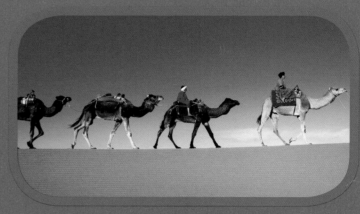

A camel train crossing the desert

River travel

Ferryboats carry people across the Congo River between the busy cities of Brazzaville and Kinshasa. On deck, people often wash clothes, cook, and look after their animals.

A crowded Congo River ferryboat

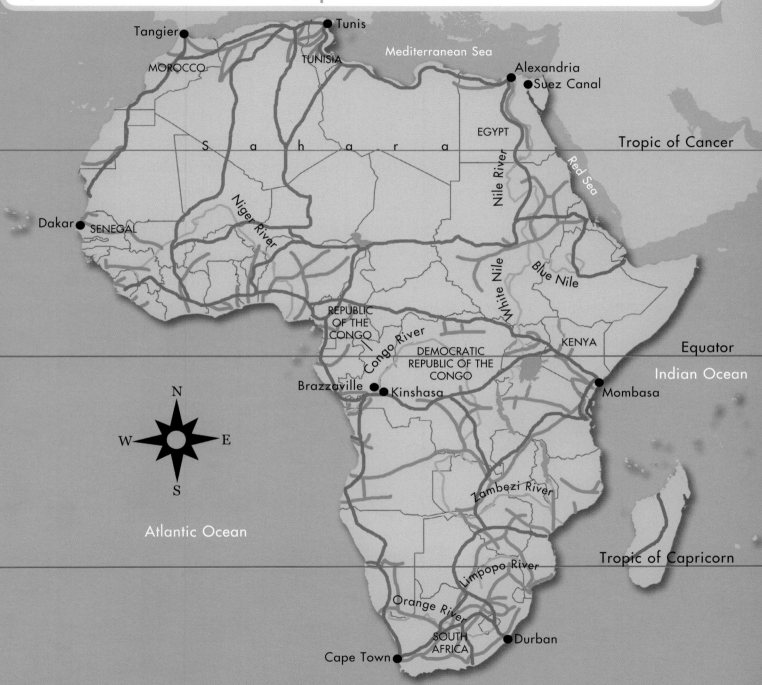

Major Transportation Routes

- ● place of interest
- —— country boundary
- —— major highway
- —— major waterway
- —— major railroad

Tangier

Tunis

MOROCCO

TUNISIA

Mediterranean Sea

Alexandria

Suez Canal

EGYPT

Tropic of Cancer

Sahara

Nile River

Red Sea

Dakar ● SENEGAL

Niger River

White Nile

Blue Nile

REPUBLIC OF THE CONGO

Congo River

DEMOCRATIC REPUBLIC OF THE CONGO

KENYA

Equator

Indian Ocean

Brazzaville ● ● Kinshasa

Mombasa

N
W E
S

Zambezi River

Atlantic Ocean

Limpopo River

Tropic of Capricorn

Orange River

SOUTH AFRICA

Durban

Cape Town

South Africa has the continent's best railway system. Its Blue Train is one of the fanciest trains in the world.

The Blue Train traveling along the coast of South Africa

Journey Across the Serengeti

The safari members start their adventure before sunrise. They take a jeep to the hot-air balloon launch site. Everyone is excited about making the flight across the Serengeti. The Serengeti is a large area of flat land, called a plain, where thousands of animals and birds live.

As the sun rises, the balloon takes off and sails above the treetops. The safari members see lions, cheetahs, and leopards out on a morning hunt.

The travelers have chosen a good time to visit. Every year, more than 1 million wildebeest and zebra migrate, or move, in herds across the Serengeti in search of fresh grasses and water. The safari members snap pictures as the balloon floats over the migrating animals.

As the balloon floats north, cattlemen look up and wave. Then the Great Rift Valley comes into view. This is where the first humans are believed to have lived 2 million years ago.

The trip is coming to the end. As the balloon flies back to base, everyone takes one long, last look at the wide plains and prepares for a bumpy landing. What a magical adventure it's been!

The Serengeti

The Serengeti covers Serengeti National Park, several other parks, and the Maasai Mara National Reserve in Kenya. More than 90,000 tourists visit Serengeti National Park each year, mainly to see the annual animal migration.

29

Africa At-a-Glance

Continent size: the second-largest of Earth's seven continents

Number of countries: 53

Major languages:

- Arabic
- English
- French
- Portuguese
- More than 1,000 Native African languages, including Swahili, Hausa, Yoruba, and Somali

Total population: 887 million (2006 estimate)

Largest country (land size): Sudan

Most populated country: Nigeria

Most populated city: Cairo, Egypt

Climate: dry in the northern region, with hot summers and warm to cold winters; tropical in the central region; dry and mild in the southern region; cool to cold in the mountains

Highest point: Mount Kilimanjaro, Tanzania, 19,340 feet (5,899 meters)

Lowest point: Lake Asal, Djibouti, 502 feet (153 m) below sea level

Longest river: Nile River

Largest body of water: Lake Victoria

Largest desert: Sahara Desert

Major agricultural products:

- bananas
- beef
- cacao beans
- cloves
- coffee
- corn
- cotton
- oil palms
- peanuts
- rice
- sheep
- tobacco

Major industries:

- mining
- agriculture
- oil
- manufacturing (consumer goods such as clothing, beverages, footwear, and soap)

Natural resources:

- bauxite
- chromium
- cobalt
- diamonds
- gold
- manganese
- oil
- platinum
- uranium

Glossary

body of water – a mass of water that is in one area; such as a river, lake, or ocean

boundary – a line that shows the border of a country, state, or other land area

climate – the average weather a place has from season to season, year to year

compass rose – a symbol used to show direction on a map

continent – one of seven large land masses on Earth, including Africa, Antarctica, Asia, Australia, Europe, North America, and South America

crops – plants that are grown in large amounts and are used for food or income

delta – the land at the mouth of a river; deltas are often shaped like triangles

desert – a hot or cold, very dry area that has few plants growing on it

dune – a hill of sand piled up by the wind

ecosystem – all of the living and nonliving things in a certain area, including plants, animals, soil, and weather

equator – an imaginary line around Earth; it divides the northern and southern hemispheres

forest – land covered by trees and plants

grassland – land covered mostly with grass

highland – high or hilly land

island – land that is completely surrounded by water

lagoon – a shallow body of water that lies near or is connected to a larger body of water

lake – a body of water that is completely surrounded by land

landform – a natural feature on Earth's surface

legend – the part of a map that explains the meaning of the map's symbols

mountain – a mass of land that rises high above the land that surrounds it

natural resources – materials such as water, trees, and minerals that are found in nature

North Pole – the northern-most point on Earth

oasis – a place in a desert that has enough water for trees and other plants to grow

ocean – the large body of saltwater that covers most of Earth's surface

peninsula – a body of land that is surrounded by water on three sides

plateau – a large, flat, and often rocky area of land that is higher than the surrounding land

population – the total number of people who live in one area

port – a place where ships can load or unload cargo (goods or people)

rain forest – a thick forest that receives a lot of rain year-round

ranching – the work of raising animals such as cattle and sheep on a ranch

river – a large stream of water that empties into a lake, ocean, or other river

scale – the size of a map or model compared to the actual size of things they stand for

South Pole – the southern-most point on Earth

temperature – how hot or cold something is

tributary – a stream or river that flows into a larger river

valley – a low place between mountains or hills

wetland – an area that has very wet soil and is covered with water at least part of the year

Index

On the Web

FactHound offers a safe, fun way to find Web sites related to topics in this book.
All of the sites on FactHound have been researched by our staff.

1. Visit *www.facthound.com*
2. Type in this special code: 1404838805
3. Click on the FETCH IT button.

Your trusty FactHound will fetch the best sites for you!

Look for all of the books in the Picture Window Books World Atlases series:

Atlas of Africa
Atlas of Australia
Atlas of Europe
Atlas of North America
Atlas of South America
Atlas of Southwest and Central Asia
Atlas of the Far East and Southeast Asia
Atlas of the Poles and Oceans